What it means to be
AWAKENED, EMPOWERED, AND ENLIGHTENED
by God

What it means to be
AWAKENED, EMPOWERED, AND ENLIGHTENED
by God

CARLTON EVANS

ARPress
ILLUMINATING IDEAS,
EMPOWERING VOICES

ARPress
45 Dan Road Suite 5
Canton MA 02021

Hotline: 1(888) 821-0229
Fax: 1(508) 545-7580

Ordering Information:
Quantity sales.Special discounts are available on quantity purchases by corporations, associations, and others.For details, contact the publisher at the address above.

Printed in the United States of America.

ISBN-13:	Paperback	979-8-89330-949-2
	eBook	979-8-89330-948-5
	Hardback	979-8-89330-952-2

Library of Congress Control Number: 2024902908

The God I encountered July 1989 is clearly described in **John 4:24 of the Holy Bible, which states, "God is Spirit: and those who worship Him must worship Him in Spirit and in Truth."** I found out firsthand that God, in His own unique way, introduces Himself to every person differently. He wants everyone to know on a personal level, in a personal way, and without any doubt that it is Him whom they have encountered. God loves everyone with a supernatural and never-ending love, but this kind of love can only be experienced when His Spirit is awakened within the core of your SOUL and His Spirit enters the SOUL when He is invited by the individual. **Revelation 3:20 of the Holy Bible reads, "Behold, I stand at the door and knock, and if anyone hears my voice and opens the door, I will come in to him, and will commune with him, and he with me."** This verse of scripture shows not only how wonderful, awesome, and powerful God is, but it also reveals how secure God is with Himself, to allow each individual the choice to invite Him into their SOUL and have a personal relationship with Him or not. I know from personal experience that God desires to have a personal and intimate relationship with everyone because this is what He gave me. This desire of God is not based on anything we have or have not done, will or will not do, but solely on His love, goodness, grace, and mercy for ALL people.

At the core of every person's SOUL resides either the human spirit or Holy Spirit. The existence of the human spirit within the SOUL is automatic within every person at birth and is without invitation according to **Psalms 51:5 of the Holy Bible,`1 which states, "Behold, I was shaped in iniquity, and in sin did my mother conceive me."** Everyone is born, shaped, and patterned after a sin-nature, which means everyone naturally does what is sinful, evil, wrong, and in

1

direct opposition to the will, desire, and intentions of God's Spirit. God desires to enter and reside within every person so we can then be conditioned, shaped, and patterned after His Holy nature. This only occurs when we are born again, born from above, or born by God's Spirit.

I am so thankful that I was born again over twenty-five years ago because from that point until this present day I have now lived, understood, embraced, and viewed life based on what is good, right, pleasing, and normal to God. I have had so many different life experiences, encounters, and relationships that confirms the fact that so many people throughout the world have never experienced what I am sharing in this book. For this reason I believe the Holy Spirit within me has led and compelled me to write this book on a very important subject in order to clearly explain how God desires His Spirit to reside within everyone, and what occurs as a result.

When the Spirit of God enters your SOUL, you become alive or awaken to God and the spirit world. In other words, God Himself and the spirit world opens up and is made real to you on a personal level and in a personal way. This is so powerful because you now realize who God is and how God has created us to exist for eternity, and how He desires us to function here on earth. You begin to know deep within that you are more than what you can only naturally comprehend and there is more to life than what you can see, taste, smell, or feel. When you receive the Spirit of God within, you begin to fully understand the purpose and meaning of life and the reason for your existence here on earth.

Over twenty-five years ago I was like so many people who believe that there is more to life than what they can see, taste, smell, or feel. I could not fully explain or understand why I felt this way but leaned that the reason this feeling exists is because there is more than what we naturally experience, but the only way to really understand this is when God reveals it to you by residing within you by His Spirit. When God's Spirit enters and resides within your SOUL, you are given spiritual eyes that allow you to see into a world that is much bigger than what you can only see with your natural eyes. When your spiritual eyes become open, you are able to see the origin, depth, plan, purpose, and meaning of life from an eternal perspective. When you are spiritually awakened, you can comprehend how important your life is to God and how He has predestined your life to be blessed, successful, safe, and secured in His presence forever. This is God's original blueprint for every individual regardless of their background, race, color, origin, gender or ethnicity.

Based on my own personal experience when the Spirit of God enters your SOUL, you experience God's overwhelming love and power deep within that is almost unexplainable. It is almost impossible to explain this supernatural experience without personally experiencing it yourself. While you can and often do physically sense something supernatural has taken place when the Spirit of God enters your SOUL, the most important part of this supernatural experience is the internal **KNOWING** that God is real and He now lives within you.

This supernatural experience does not stop here or end after this initial experience, because God now resides within you. Many people have heard someone talk about coming out of darkness and entering into the marvelous light and many have also heard someone talk about being lost but now found, was blind, but now they can see. This is literally what I experienced when the Spirit of God came into my SOUL. When I asked God this question, "God, if you are real, show yourself to me and let know you exist." Jesus Christ, through the power of God's Spirit, immediately entered my SOUL in my barracks room at Fort Bragg, North Carolina. My room suddenly lit up with a bright flash of light even though my room was physically dark. It was an instant quick flash of bright light that took over both the spiritual and the physical darkness. I could now spiritually see what I could not see before, and at that point I experienced the reality of God's supernatural presence and power on the inside of me.

What was so powerful about this experience is that nobody had to tell me it was God that I just encountered because I knew for myself personally that I had just met the only true and living God for the first time in my life at twenty-one years of age. Along with the bright flash of light shining in my room, I could physically feel all my cares, worries, concerns, doubts, uncertainties, insecurities, and questions leave my life. The Spirit of God during this experience was so powerful and overwhelming that I could literally feel God removing all the bad, negative, and evil things from my life in exchange for what I had always searched for, wanted, and needed that no words could fully explain. One thing I knew for certain is that I just met God and no one would ever be able to convince me otherwise.

I am so thankful to God for revealing Himself to me and giving me the opportunity to invite Him into my SOUL. **I Peter 2:9 of the Holy Bible reads, "But ye are a chosen generation, a royal priesthood, a holy nation, a special people, that ye should show forth the praises of Him who has called you out of darkness into His marvelous light."** The marvelous light the Bible is talking about is the light of God's glory, presence, and reality, which I experienced is not a physical light but is God completely expressing Himself. God's marvelous light removes the ignorance, darkness, and sin that is within **ALL** of us, which is the unknowing, and lack of having a personal experience with God. When the Spirit of God entered my SOUL, my entire inner person, my core, the totality of my being was awakened, empowered, and enlightened. At that very moment I knew for the first time in my life who I really was, not who I thought I was, or told by the world, my family, or my friends who I was. I began to clearly understand I was meant to be here on earth and why. The only way this could have happened to me and made known to me is by asking and then inviting God's Spirit within. No matter where you are from, your race, ethnicity, social status, education level, affiliations, connections, amount of money you have, or do not have what I am sharing in this book can only become a reality in your life is by God's Spirit. Let me ask you an honest question. Wherever you are in your life right now, can you say with one hundred percent sincerity, certainty, humility, and honesty that you really know who you are, why you are here on earth, and where you will spend your life for eternity? I know that many people cannot say yes to these questions, but you can change that any day, time, or location by receiving the Spirit of God within your SOUL. God's Holy Spirit reveals who you are, why you are here, and His eternal will, plan, and purpose for your life, and I can tell you that this is a very comforting and assuring feeling to be able to answer yes to these questions.

II Corinthians 5:17 of the Holy Bible states, "If any person is in a relationship with Jesus Christ, they are a new creature, old things are passed away, BEHOLD, all things are made new." When the Spirit of God enters your SOUL, He begins to lead, develop, prosper, govern, and protect your life from the inside out and not from the outside in. The Spirit of God will lead and guide you in the direction you're intended to go according to God, which is a preordained and preplanned path of blessing, prosperity, and goodness while here on earth, and for eternity. **Psalms 119:105 of the Holy Bible states, "Thy word is a lamp unto my feet and light unto my path."** This means that the Spirit of God reveals to you where you are in life and then directs your life. **Romans 8:14 of the Holy Bible states, "For as many as are led by the Spirit of God, they are the sons of God."** This speaks to the fact that when the Spirit of God enters your SOUL, you become His son, which is not a natural transformation or process, but a spiritual one. When this occurs, God begins to relate with you as a natural father should with his natural son. When the Spirit of God enters you into your SOUL, He now becomes your Heavenly Father. **Romans 8:15 of the Holy Bible states, "For you have not received spiritual bondage and captivity again, but you have received this Spirit of adoption unto God, crying Abba Father."** Being in a relationship with God comes down to belief and faith. God the Father only accepts belief and faith in Him in a personal and intimate way.

Hebrews 11:6 of the Holy Bible states, "But without faith it is impossible to please God, for He that cometh to God must believe that He is, and that He rewards them that diligently seek Him." Being in a relationship with God may sound like something mysterious, difficult, impossible, or unrealistic. But once you know Him, you know that God wants a relationship with you more than you do. He begins leading you in the direction and to the places He desires you to go. I remember when I was very young I always thought I would be a professional athlete because I was a very good in several sports. I gave so much time, energy, and attention to athletics because that was pretty much all I knew and saw others do around me, but through a series of different events, circumstances, and situations, both positive and negative, I noticed my passions and desires were beginning to change starting mostly during my high school years and during my brief time in college before I enlisted in the United States Army. For all the veterans out there, please do not read into what I am going to say in a negative way because I am only driving home a spiritual point. I honestly never gave any thought of enlisting in the Military growing up because I did not see the Military within my personality, demeanor, mind-set, and attitude, the environments in which I grew up. I did not think I would last long in the Military because of these factors, but I can look back and can say now that enlisting in the Army was one of the best things that ever happened to me. It got me out of the environment I was conditioned by and God began to use many different people, experiences, locations, and assignments throughout my career as part of His spiritual development, teaching, mentoring, shaping, and maturation process. As I look back, I cannot thank God enough for how He masterfully and wonderfully used my twenty-one years of United States Army service to do what He desired and wanted to do in, for, and through me. Even though I did not or could not understand this back then, but I do now because now I know. I can now say that I would not have wanted to experience my life any other way, because it has been all by God's Spirit in my life.

God knows what He wants out of **ALL** our lives because He created us and He strategically places us where He wants us to be and what He wants us to do in His time and season. **Ecclesiastes 3:1 of the Holy Bible states, "To everything there is a season and a time to every purpose under heaven."** Our lives have already been established, preordained, and prearranged by God before we were born to be blessed, successful, and prosperous, and not cursed or bad. **Jeremiah 29:11 of the Holy Bible states, "For I know the thoughts I think toward you, says the Lord, thoughts of peace and not of evil to give you an expected end."**

Before I met God personally, I did not know He thought this way about me. To be honest, I did not know what God thought about me or what He already had prepared for me before the foundation of the world, but once I met God and after reading **Jeremiah 29:11**, I fully understood why God thought this way about me. Let us pause and think about this for a moment. Why would God, who created us, think about us any other way? God only loves, blesses, and prospers **ALL** of us, but the devil, who is the origin of sin and evil, is the one who causes us to think differently than the way we should about God, ourselves, and others. Again, God only wants us to think and live like Him! **Romans 6:23 states, "For the wages of sin is death but the gift of God is eternal life through Jesus Christ our Lord."** I knew very quickly when I met God that He was giving me a free gift that He really wanted me to receive and it was not based on anything I did or did not do, but solely on the fact that He always has and always will love me. I openly, without reservation or hesitation, received this free gift of salvation through His only begotten Son Jesus Christ, which was just the beginning of my personal and intimate relationship and journey with Him. I still realize to this day that God is within me, not based on what I do or do not do but solely because His love and grace, the only way you can fully understand and comprehend what I am sharing is by receiving His Spirit within your SOUL. When God's Spirit lives within you, He confirms and reaffirms the depths of His love, plan, and purpose for whoever chooses to believe and have faith in Him.

I want to share something God showed me years ago that I often share in conversations or when teaching. In many ways, life seems to be like giant a puzzle where there are many different pieces, and they seem to be all out of place, disconnected from one another, and do not seem to be able to come together. However when you have a relationship with God, you begin to see with your spiritual eyes His mighty and glorious Holy Spirit moving all the pieces of your life into place perfectly, with precision and accuracy. As this occurs, you develop clearer vision, clearer perspective, and clearer perception about God and your personal life as well as the life of others. This is crucial when it comes to how we experience life while here on earth. As you live each day with this new eternal point of view, you begin to experience life the way God has always intended you to. What do I mean by this? This is when you live from a high place within a place of spiritual awareness, discernment, and comprehension.

You are now able to see as God sees, believe how God wants to believe, do what God wants you do, say what God wants you to say, and have what God wants you to have! When you look at how the prophet Jeremiah's life was established by God in **Jeremiah chapter one**, God gave and ensured Jeremiah the spiritual sight he needed in order to have the right point of view of himself and the world. He would need this spiritual sight in order to live out the plan and purpose for which God placed Him on the earth for. As it was for Jeremiah, so it for us. Until the Spirit of God enters your SOUL, you will not be able to function and operate like this while here on earth. Yes, you heard that correctly function and operate like God here on earth!

Genesis 1:26 of the Holy Bible states, "And God said, let us make man in our image, after our likeness, and then have dominion over the fish of the sea, and over the fowl of air, and over the cattle, and over all the earth (not people), over every living thing that moves upon the earth." Also, John 4:17 of the Holy Bible states, "And as we live in God, our love grow more perfect. So we will not be afraid on the day of final judgment, but we can face Him with confidence because as He is, so are we in this world." As you can see, God wants us to function and operate like Him here on earth. How? By representing, reflecting, and reproducing His spiritual nature and characteristics. This can ONLY happen when His Spirit resides within you.

Before I met God personally I did not think or act this way, nor did I have any idea nor any way of knowing I could. It is absolutely impossible to live and function this way apart from God's Spirit.

Zachariah 4:6 of the Holy Bible states, "Then He answered and spoke unto me saying, this is the word of the Lord unto Zerubbabel, saying, it is not by might, not by power, but by my Holy Spirit, says the Lord." Just as the Spirit of God leads us, He also perfects or matures us. When the Spirit of God dwells within your SOUL, He perfects or matures you, which means He is continually transforming you into becoming more and more like Himself. True maturity has nothing to do with your age, success, achievements, social status, titles, positions, or accumulation of money and material things, but it is in our ability to surrender, yield, and submit totally to God's Spirit.

Hebrews 5:12–14 states, "For when the time ye ought to be teachers, ye have need that one teach you again the first principles of the oracles of God, and become such as have need of milk, and not of strong meat. For everyone that uses milk is unskillful in the work of righteousness for he is a baby. But strong meat belongs to them that are of full age (mature), even those who by reason of use have their senses exercised to discern both good and evil." One of the most important attributes and characteristics that prove the Spirit of God is within you, is having the ability to discern or differentiate between good and evil.

Another way that proves that you are or are not spiritually maturing is how you relate with people and how you handle issues and challenges that come with everyday life, and the results or outcomes of your life based on the decisions you make. All this proves whether you are or not spiritually maturing. If your life stays in a place of constant defeat, suffering, loss, failure and not experiencing the promises of God, then you know you are not discerning the root causes, which is a clear sign that you are not spiritually maturing. The devil attacks **ALL** of us but the difference is our ability to recognize his strategies and attacks, and then be able to change them from defeats, into victories. Being able to discern between good and evil, is without a doubt, a clear sign of spiritual maturity that manifests in our lives every day as well as our ability to make wise decisions. I am so thankful that the Spirit of God within me constantly perfects and matures me. This spiritual process has and never will stop, as it continues each and every day of my life. In other words, because God's Spirit is within me I continue to live better and make better decisions on this spiritual journey with God. The Spirit of God within has enabled me to make wise and decisive decisions that have produced God's results in my and my family's. My family continues to see positive spiritual change, growth, and progress as we continue seeking and desiring God.

When the Spirit of God is within you, He brings clarity to your mind and your thoughts, or another way of putting it your mind's eye. This enables you to see into, through, above, and beyond this physical world. You are now able to see the bigger picture. When you are able to do this, you can make decisions more confidently producing God's results in your life and in the life of others. As I look at the many things that are taking place throughout the world today, particularly here in America, it is obvious that many people do not know how to make wise, quality, and decisive decisions that produce positive results for themselves and for those around them.

Whenever God's Spirit is within you, you are given supernatural judgment and discretion. This should be normal for every believer because this comes from God's Spirit. When God is not within your SOUL, you are not capable of fully functioning or operating with sound judgment or discretion. Whenever an individual does not possess wisdom, discernment, and sound judgment, someone is going to be negatively impacted because of what they say or do. Many people throughout the world today, act and speak without thinking first, which reveals they lack wisdom, discernment, discretion, and sound judgment.

Proverbs 4:7 of the Holy Bible states, "Wisdom is the principle thing therefore get wisdom and with all thy getting, get understanding." When the Spirit of God is within you, He enables you to make the godly decisions, which are right and good, for yourself and others. Having the ability to make godly decisions is so important because this keeps you from making decisions that cost you and others spiritual, psychological, emotional, and even in many cases, financial problems. Receiving the Spirit of God within guarantees that you have the ability and opportunity to make clear, wise, and decisive godly decisions in your life, each and everyday.

Another important spiritual attribute and characteristic I now possess is the ability to comprehend or understand correctly. I now have the right mind-set, mentality, perspective, and point of view of myself, my family, and the world as a whole. **2 Corinthians 4:3–4 of the Holy Bible states, "But if our good news be hid, it is hid from them that are lost. In whom the god of this world (the devil) has blinded the minds of them that do not believe, unless the light of the glorious**

good news of Jesus Christ who is the image of God should shine in them." The Spirit of God within has made me spiritually and sober-minded, solid in my thinking and thought processes. I can tell you from firsthand experience that solid or sober thinking produces a solid and stable life.

So many people today are very unstable, wishy-washy, and go in whatever direction the wind blows. They are double-minded because they have been conformed to the spirit of this world and have not been filled with the Spirit of God. Thus, the only direction they can go in is whatever direction the spiritual winds of this world take them. **Romans 12:2 states, "And be not conformed to this world but be transformed by the renewing of your mind, that ye may prove what is that good, acceptable, and perfect will of God."** An easy way to know what I am sharing is true is just by listening to how most people talk today, what they talk about, what they focus on, and what they give their time and attention to. This is exactly where the devil had me until I received the Spirit of God within.

God creates everyone to be good and pleasing in His sight, but the devil perverts, twists, and distorts what God creates to be good and pleasing in His sight into something bad and wrong. The devil wants every person to see themselves, others, and the world as a whole, from his evil perspective. This is why there is so much evil, hatred, division, ill-will, wrong motives, envy, jealousy, strife, back-biting, gossip, chaos, and confusion in the world today. God's desire is for everyone to love, honor, respect, exalt, build up, promote, and encourage one another on the basis of our personal and intimate relationship with Him.

Many people today believe more in the devil's false reality rather than God's true reality. You might be asking why is this the case? When the Spirit of God illuminated and enlightened my mind's eye back in July 1989 where my spiritual journey began, the ability to think right, think things through, analyze things properly, and see things on the basis of God's Spirit. I have a question I would like to ask you with all sincerity, truth, and love. Are you living in a personal and intimate relationship with God today? Are you walking on God's path and journey today, and going in God's direction? God's Spirit within you enables and empowers you to live God's way, experiencing God's results. His Spirit keeps you walking and staying on His path for your life, and know for sure that you are going in His direction. **Matthew 7:13–14 of the Holy Bible states, "Enter at the strait gate, for wide is the gate and broad is the way that lead to destruction and many be that go there after, because strait is the gate and narrow is the way, which leads to life and few be that find it."** The Spirit of God within is who clearly leads and guides your life step-by-step, each and every day, so you know where you are and where you are supposed to go. **John 14:26 of the Holy Bible states, "But the Helper, the Holy Spirit, whom the Father will send in my name, He will teach you all things and bring to your remembrance all things that I said to you." Proverbs 14:12 states, "There is a way, which seems right to a man but the end is the way of death."** God has a blessed and prosperous way that is already established for you but the devil has a destructive way for your life, and you personally have to know and decide which path you want to follow. I am thankful to God for giving me His Spirit within so I know I am being led by His Spirit to the places where I could not take myself at the appointed time and season I am supposed to arrive there.

When you have the Spirit of God within, you know He is leading you to the places that no man can stop you from arriving to, because God opens doors that no man can close and closes doors that no man can open. In other words, God's Spirit ensures we will arrive at the destination He plans for us to arrive at. I have personally experienced and witnessed so many times since receiving the Spirit of God within. How God has taken me to the places He wants me to take me, which is where I should be rather than where I would have on my own. For this reason I want to pause and say, "Thank you, God, because you have proven yourself to be God in every aspect of my life over and over again! When the Spirit of God is within, you can clearly see the paths that are in front of you and discern if it is blessed or cursed. But if you do not have the Spirit of God within, you cannot clearly see if the paths that are in front of you are either blessed or cursed. The devil wants you to be lost, unsure, indecisive, and in darkness concerning your life. He had me on this path of destruction and eternal death from birth until July 1989 when I could not clearly see that I was on the wrong path, but the results my life revealed that I was in fact on the wrong path. Once I knew I was on the wrong path, the real issue then was how do I get off this wrong path and get on the right path. This was the deception the devil had my life trapped in but when the Spirit of God came inside of me, I was not only able to see I was on the wrong path I was able to see the path that I needed to get on and get on it. Thank you, Father!

Many people know or believe they are on the wrong path for their life. They also do not know that they can or how to get off the wrong path, and get on the right path. Also, there are those who do not know they are on the wrong path so they would not know or don't care to even think of getting off the wrong path and getting on the right path. Many people today, particularly politicians and those in the media, welcome, accommodate, push, endorse and promote sin and evil under what has been termed "political correctness." This is clearly a strategy of the devil because it comes from the human spirit and not from the Spirit of God. "Political correctness" is a demonic tool used by politicians and the media to make their lies and hypocrisy sound and seem legitimate in order to get people to believe and support them. According to the Holy Bible there are only two ways in life, God's way or the devil's way.

Sorry for that brief tangent but I wanted to show how the Spirit of God within enables you to see through a very real and prevalent evil in our country today. Lies and deception always incarcerates and traps people, but truth always sets people free. Which spiritual path are you on in your life today? If you know that you are not on the right path, why don't you get on the right path today? If you do not know that you are on the right path but want to be sure, ask God and He will reveal it to you. **2 Peter 3:9 of the Holy Bible states, "The Lord is not slack concerning His promise, as some men count slackness, but is longsuffering toward us all not willing that any should perish but that all should come to repentance."**

The fruit that your life produces is the proof that reveals if you are on the right or wrong path. **Matthew 7:20 of the Holy Bible states, "Wherefore by their fruits ye shall know them."**

Ultimately my life and your life is not about what we say or how we present ourselves publicly, it is about what our lives produce and how it impacts ourselves and others. This is what **Matthew 7:20 states, "Wherefore, by their fruit you will know them."** If your mind has not been renewed by the Word of God, your life will not produce Godly fruit. I am thankful that my life now produces Godly fruit, but it did not up until July 1989. I said and did a lot of things prior to July 1989 that did not produce God's results. I was just like so many people before receiving the Spirit of God within. I did things for short-term and unproductive self-gratification, which produced problems for me and those who I interacted with. No matter what anyone feels or thinks, sin has consequences that ultimately result in spiritual and often physical death. However, salvation produces spiritual life and, often, even physical blessings. Why would anyone not want this? But unfortunately this is the reality for so many people in the world today. So many people are experiencing so many problems, issues, confusion, chaos, dysfunction, destruction, and death. The root cause of this always was and still is sin. It amazes me to hear and see so many people trying to come up with their own plans, solutions, methods, and programs to solve problems. Since the root cause of these problems is sin, the only answer for them is salvation through Jesus Christ. All the problems and issues people are having and what we are seeing throughout the world are really spiritual problems! This is where the challenge is, because so many people do not understand or believe this, because they do not have the Spirit of God within.

The many problems we see are so obvious to everyone, but the fact of the matter is the way most try to solve them is not working and does not produce quality results. **The universal meanings of the word 'insanity' is doing the same thing over and over again, expecting different results.** You have to ask why so many people refuse to change what they are doing that does not work but still expect to get good results? In order for real change to take place in anyone's life, change must first take place within one's SOUL. Many people either do not know or believe that change must first take place within their SOUL because if they did, they would do things differently to get a different results. **Proverbs 23:7 of the Holy Bible states, "For as a man thinks in his SOUL, so is he."** What this means is that we are who we are and have what we have is based on how we think. In other words, we are what we think!This is why we must continue to allow our minds to be renewed by the Word of God through His Spirit. At this point I want to ask you to take this brief self-examination. On a scale of one to ten, where is your life in theses following areas:

Internal Well-Being (Soul)   _____

Physical Well-Being (Body)   _____

Quality of Relationships   _____

Financial Status   _____

Employment/ Business Status   _____

How did your results turn out? This brief self-examination is not designed to embarrass or expose you so please keep your responses to yourself, but think about your answers in terms of what you do not like, realizing that what you do not like can only change when the Spirit of God is within you. At some point in all of our lives we must experience a spiritual awakening, an awakening to the reality of God Himself. After this awakening happened in my life, I could see that I lived two completely different lives. I lived a life without God and then began to live to a life with God. I am now able to clearly see and understand that while He was always there trying to show me this and get me to know His love, grace, mercy, kindness, prosperity, and protection, I could not see it without His Spirit inside of me. I could not and did not see this before I met Him but if I could have, I would have wanted to know Him a long time ago. But I can joyfully say that because I now have His eternal reality in my life, I know there is a clear difference. So many people only know one side of this equation, the side without knowing Him on a personal level and in a personal way by His Spirit and this is very unfortunate. The Spirit of God within lets you know and reminds you that you are intimate and secure with God, and He is with you and is for you.

I am going to say something that many may disagree with but the fact is even when you do something wrong, bad, sinful, and evil, if you have personally met God and have an intimate relationship with Him, He still loves you the same and without any condemnation in spite of the wrong we do. But, again, this does not mean that there are no consequences for the wrong we do but God still continues to show you His overwhelming and never-ending love in spite of our wrongs, bad behavior, sin, and evil, because this is who He is. This does not mean we do not suffer for wrong, but this does not change our relationship with Him. This is what moves my SOUL all the time and makes me want to please God and allow Him to have free access to my life without any reservations or resistance. Nobody else can love you like God can and many times it is really difficult to explain this kind of love and relationship to others, because even when you are living in a way that displeases God He does not respond to you like the average person does. God always responds to us in such a way that if we really think about ourselves or someone else in comparison to Him, we are left speechless and without any reason to not want to be full of His Spirit and His presence.

Genesis 3:8–9 of the Holy Bible states, "Then the man (Adam) and his wife (Eve) heard the sound of the Lord God as He was walking in the Garden of Eden in the cool of the day, and they hid from the Lord God among the trees of the garden. But the Lord God called to the man, 'Where are you?'" This event occurred after Adam and Eve sinned in the Garden of Eden by eating the forbidden fruit causing both of them to hide and be separated from God's presence. Prior to committing this sin, being in God's presence for Adam and Eve was just as normal as breathing. Even though they sinned and tried to hide themselves from God's presence, God still pursued them because He only desires to be in an intimate relationship with His creation. Even though Adam and Eve would suffer consequences and pay a great price for their sin, God's love for them never changed. When God's Spirit is within you, you know and understand this kind of love. But when you do not, you cannot know or understand this kind of love. Therefore you have to remember this very important point, the only way you can be in and stay in God's presence experiencing this kind

16

of supernatural and never-ending love is by having His Spirit within your SOUL. **The Holy Bible states in John 4:24, "God is Spirit and those who worship Him must worship Him in Spirit and in Truth." Also, Psalm 16:11 says, "You will show me the path of life. In your presence is fullness of joy, and in your right hand are pleasures forever more."**

The only place God ever wants **ALL** of us to be is in His presence, both now while here on earth and forever in eternity. This is what God revealed to me when I had an encounter with Him over twenty-five years ago. If God would introduce Himself to me so personally with the fact that there are so many others here on earth, then why would He stay away from me or hide from me? He never has, nor ever will, do this to anyone. Praise God! **Deuteronomy 31:6 of the Holy Bible states, "Be strong and courageous and do not be afraid or terrified because of them, for the Lord your God is with you and He will never leave you nor forsake you."** God cannot and will not leave you or forsake you.

I have learned that God, in His unique and masterful way, always lets you know that He is with you. He does things in various and mysterious ways to let you know it is Him. He has always been and always will be there for me and He will always be there for you. I am confident of this! Natural situations, circumstances, and problems that go on all around us often makes it seem like God is not there but trust me, He is always there. **Psalm 37:25 states, "I was young and now I am old, yet I have never seen the righteous forsaken nor his seed begging for bread."**

When you are filled with God's Spirit, you have spiritual courage, confidence, security, and peace. **Philippians 4:7 of the Holy Bible states, "And the peace of God, which passes all understanding shall keep your heart and mind through Christ Jesus."** Having this kind of inner spiritual courage, confidence, security, and peace in my life, blesses me every day. The only way I know that what I am sharing is real and present in my life is because the Spirit of God is within me.

17

II Timothy 3:16 states, "All scripture is given by inspiration of God, and is profitable for doctrine, for reproof, for correction, and for instruction in righteousness." Once I received the Spirit of God within, I received the ability to understand, interpret, and rightly divide or, in other words, accurately know what the Holy Bible means in its proper context. Knowing God for over the past twenty-five years, I have learned that many people do not clearly understand the Holy Bible in its context. The Holy Bible is the most important physical element we need for living a victorious and prosperous life here on earth. The Holy Bible is the foundation, guide, and final authority for those who say they are believers, disciples of Jesus Christ, and children of God the Father. There is absolutely no way anyone can understand a spiritual book without the Holy Spirit within them, because it was birthed and breathed into existence by God's Spirit according to the Holy Bible. The Holy Bible is the law, statute, commandment, governing principles, and standard of God for everyone, whether they choose to believe it or not.

To this day, the Holy Bible is the most read, most purchased, and still the most important book in the entire world! When you look at your individual life and the world around you from the Holy Bible's perspective or point of view, you see the clear contrasts between good vs. evil and right vs. wrong. Something I shared earlier that needs to be reiterated here, is when people who live out of their human spirit will **ALWAYS** be in direct opposition and contrast to the Holy Spirit, until they are born again or born from above.

For you who are reading this book hopefully know that what God says in His Holy Bible is good and right, but so many people today are saying by their behavior and lifestyle, it is evil or wrong. What God says is always good and right! **Isaiah 5:20–24 of the Holy Bible states, "Woe to them that call evil good and good evil, that put darkness for light and light for darkness, that put bitter for sweet and sweet for bitter. Woe to them that are wise in their own eyes and prudent in their own sight. Woe unto them that are mighty to drink and men of strength to mingle with strong drink. Which justify the wicked for reward and take away the righteousness of the righteous from him who believes? Therefore, as the fire**

18

devours the stubble and the flame consumes the chaff, so their root shall be as rottenness, and their blossom shall go up like dust, because they have cast away the law of the Lord of hosts and despised the word of the Holy One of Israel." Also, Romans 1:25 of the Holy Bible states, "Who changed the truth of God into a lie and worshipped and served the creature more that the Creator, who is blessed forever."

What I have learned is that whenever the Spirit of God is not within an individual, that individual is incapable of fully knowing, believing, and living for God. Again, the Holy Bible is the foundation, law, statute, commandment, and governing principles, and standard for everyone. And if you do not believe this, your life is destined for problems, destruction, and ultimate spiritual death. God gave our world His Holy Bible so we would have written physical evidence that He is the only true and living God and He exists. That means by His very character and nature, we can live victorious and prosperous while here on the earth and experience the blessings and rewards He promised if we believe it!

Luke 21:33 of the Holy Bible states, "Heaven and earth shall pass away but my words shall never pass away." You may have read or heard someone quote scripture verses in your lifetime but this passage of scripture is one of, if not, the most powerful verses of scripture in the entire Holy Bible, because God is telling all mankind that the only words that matter are His words. While God still speaks and reveals His eternal words to us by His Spirit, nothing He will ever speak or reveal to us will violate what is written in His Holy Bible. You have to have a personal desire to want to get to the place in your relationship with God where His words and ways are all that matter to you. I am so thankful that I have gotten to this place in my relationship with God of complete and confident belief, trust, and faith in His words. How did this happen? It happened because His Spirit is within me.

II Corinthians 3:6 of the Holy Bible states, "Who also hath made us able ministers of the new testament not of the letter but of the Holy Spirit; for the letter kills but the Holy Spirit gives life." You have to understand that the Holy Bible by itself is nothing and means

19

nothing and cannot be fully comprehended without God's Spirit. The Holy Bible is a living book because of the Holy Spirit. Therefore, wherever the Holy Spirit is there is eternal life. When our lives are built and established upon the Holy Bible through the authority and power of God's Spirit, we are in agreement and harmony with the Heavenly Father and we will conquer and experience victory right here on earth.

Jesus Christ knew His life was in complete agreement and harmony with God so He conquered and experienced victory while He was here on earth because His life was built and established upon the Holy Bible through the authority and power of the Holy Spirit. Look at what the Holy Bible states in **Matthew 4:3–4, "And when the temper came to him, he said, 'If thou be the Son of God, command that these stones be made bread.' But Jesus answered and said, 'IT IS WRITTEN, man shall not live by bread alone but by every word that proceeds out of the mouth of God.'"** If Jesus' life and ministry was established upon the Holy Bible, through the authority and power of God's Spirit, how must we live? We have to and should want to live the same way Jesus Christ did while He was here on earth because when we do, we experience life the same way He did, which was conquering a victorious life. I have spent a lot of time in this area because it is the most important area we must understand in order to function and operate in our lives each and every day. The most important thing you have to remember is, you can only fully understand the Holy Bible when the Spirit of God dwells within you, and once you do begin to understand and comprehend the Holy Bible, you will be able to apply it to your life accurately with wisdom, confidence, and faith, which will cause the promises of God to manifest in your life right here on earth.

What I am going to share next is very important as well, because I am sharing the importance of personally receiving and embracing truth especially when it comes to how to love people but simultaneously hating sin. This is probably one of the most important revelations that many people do not fully understand and live out in the world today. The fact that I have heard so many people throughout the course of my life say and do things that prove they do not fully understand this revelation and its importance. I am so thankful to God for receiving this revelation many years ago, because it has helped me know how to properly relate and deal with people. God loves every person the same, no more or no less than anyone else, period! It is not based on anything you have or have not done, will or will not do, but at the same time He does hate and judge sin and evil. Why would God hate anyone whom He created?He does not! He hates sin and evil because He knows it keeps people separated and apart from Him, both while here on the earth and it will for all eternity. **John 3:16 states, "For God so loved the world that He gave His only begotten Son, that whoever believes in Him will not perish but have eternal life." 2 Peter 3:9, "The Lord is not slack concerning his promise, as some people count slackness, but is longsuffering toward us not willing that anyone should perish, but that all should come to repentance."**

What God is saying in these verses of scripture is that because of His never-ending love for you, His desire is that you be in and stay in a personal and intimate relationship with Him your entire life. You cannot keep going in a direction away from Him, so make the decision to turn to Him and draw near to Him, if you have not already. Because once you do this, you can live daily in His presence and prosper and have the fullness of joy!

The only reason I kept going away from God was because I did not personally know who He is, how much He loves me, and how much He wanted to have a personal and intimate relationship with me. Most people do not know this or even believe that they too can be in a personal and intimate relationship with God. The only thing that kept me and keeps anyone from being in a personal and intimate relationship with Him is sin! Sin is anything that keeps you separated from God's glory, presence, and love. This is why God created us and where He wants **ALL** of us to be with Him. God's Spirit within me allows me to know Him more and more each and every day. And as a result of knowing Him more and more, He lets me know more and more who I am and why I am here. This is a supernatural revelation from God to me, because He does not want me or anyone to not know Him. **ALL** of us are here to worship and glorify God!

What I shared in this book cannot and will not happen through pursuing or obtaining great fame, status, degrees, accumulation of money, personal accomplishments, through manmade laws of self-interests, politicians or politics, or success, as defined by the world. What I shared in this book is a personal glimpse of some very important keys that completely transformed my life. I know that the world will try almost any and everything to find fulfillment, satisfaction, and solutions for their many questions except through knowing the only true and living God, who is Spirit. Just remember this, God can only be known by His Spirit being within your SOUL. So invite and accept Him into your life through His only begotten son Jesus Christ, which is to be born again or from above by His Spirit. Amen!

Carlton Christ Evans Jr.

United States Army (Retired)

Master of Science in Management from Strayer University

Bachelor of Science in Organizational Leadership from Nyack College

Contact Information:

(571) 286-7969 or evanspraise@verizon.net

www.ingramcontent.com/pod-product-compliance
Lightning Source LLC
Chambersburg PA
CBHW041629140626
46547CB00031B/1931